BED RUNNERS
& more™

Edited by Carolyn S. Vagts

HOUSE of WHITE BIRCHES
PUBLISHERS
SINCE 1947

Introduction

Sometimes all a room needs is a few fresh accents to give it a whole new look—a couple of pillows, a change of curtains or a coat of paint. For a quilter, a new bed runner and a set of matching pillow shams are all you need to make it happen.

The bed is the focal point of the bedroom, so what better way to make your own creative statement than with one of the bed runners and/or shams from this book? You could even change the look of your bed with the seasons, if you wished.

Once again, our talented designers have created stunning projects just for you. Within the pages of this book you will find a collection of unique and attractive bed runners and pillow shams. There is something for everyone. Imagine these clever designs in your colors on your bed.

You will find nine runners—six with matching shams in a variety of both Euro or standard-size shams. Let the possibilities inspire you. Make your bedroom shine.

I hope you enjoy this book as much as I have.

Happy quilting!

Carolyn

Table of Contents

Warm Splendor,
page 38

Winter Wonderland,
page 48

Geometric Jazz

Designs by Carol Zentgraf

A bed runner with matching shams makes
great use of solids for a contemporary look.

Project Specifications
Skill Level: Beginner
Bed Runner Size: 67" x 30"
Sham Size: 27" x 20½"
Block Size: 20" x 13"
Number of Blocks: 8

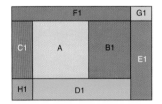

Geometric Jazz 1
20" x 13" Block
Make 4

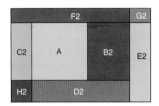

Geometric Jazz 2
20" x 13" Block
Make 4

Materials
- ⅓ yard brown solid
- ⅓ yard yellow solid
- ½ yard turquoise solid
- ½ yard green solid
- ½ yard slate blue tonal
- ⅝ yard slate blue solid
- ⅝ yard tan solid
- ¾ yard persimmon solid
- 1⅔ yards muslin
- 1⅞ yards persimmon print
- Backing 75" x 38"

- Low-loft batting: 75" x 38" (runner),
  (2) 35" x 28" (shams)
- All-purpose thread to match fabrics
- Quilting thread
- Basic sewing tools and supplies

Cutting
1. Cut two 8½" by fabric width strips tan solid; subcut strip into eight 8½" A squares.

2. Cut one 6½" by fabric width strip persimmon solid; subcut strip into four 6½" x 8½" B1 rectangles.

3. Cut two 2½" by fabric width strips persimmon solid; subcut strips into four 2½" x 17½" F1 strips.

4. Cut two 4½" by fabric width strips persimmon solid; subcut strips into three 4½" x 20½" I strips.

5. Cut one 3½" by fabric width strip green solid; subcut strip into four 3½" x 8½" C1 strips.

6. Cut two 3½" by fabric width strips green solid; subcut strips into four 3½" x 14½" D2 strips.

7. Cut one 3½" by fabric width strip turquoise solid; subcut strip into four 3½" x 8½" C2 strips.

8. Cut two 3½" by fabric width strips turquoise solid; subcut strips into four 3½" x 14½" D1 strips.

9. Cut two 3½" by fabric width strips brown solid; subcut strips into four 3½" x 11½" E1 strips and four 3½" x 2½" G2 rectangles.

10. Cut two 3½" by fabric width strips yellow solid; subcut strips into four 3½" x 11½" E2 strips, four 3½" x 2½" G1 rectangles and two 3½" x 4" M rectangles.

11. Cut one 6½" by fabric width strip slate blue solid; subcut strip into four 6½" x 8½" B2 rectangles.

12. Cut two 2½" by fabric width strips slate blue solid; subcut strips into four 2½" x 17½" F2 strips.

House of White Birches, Berne, Indiana 46711   Clotilde.com

13. Cut one 4½" by fabric width strip slate blue solid; subcut strip into two 4½" x 20½" K strips.

14. Cut two 4" by fabric width strips persimmon print; subcut strips into two 4" x 14" L strips and two 4" x 17½" N2 strips. Trim the remainder of the strip to 3½" and cut four 3½" H1 squares.

15. Cut two 2¼" by fabric width strips persimmon print; subcut strips into two 2¼" x 27½" O2 strips.

16. Cut two 17" by fabric width strips persimmon print; subcut strips into four 17" x 21" rectangles for sham backs.

17. Cut five 2¼" by fabric width strips persimmon print for binding.

18. Cut two 4" by fabric width strips slate blue tonal; subcut strips into two 4" x 14" J strips and two 4" x 17½" N1 strips. Trim the remainder of the strip to 3½" and cut four 3½" H2 squares.

19. Cut two 2¼" by fabric width strips slate blue tonal; subcut strips into two 2¼" x 27½" O1 strips.

20. Cut two 35" x 28" rectangles muslin for sham-top backings.

Completing the Blocks

1. To make one Geometric Jazz 1 block, select one each A and B1–H1 pieces.

2. Sew A to B1; press seam toward B1.

3. Referring to Figure 1, sew D1 to the A-B1 unit; press seam toward D1. Add E1 and press seam toward E1.

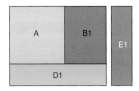

Figure 1

4. Sew H1 to C1; press seam toward C1. Add the C1-H1 unit to the previously pieced unit as shown in Figure 2; press seam toward the C1-H1 unit.

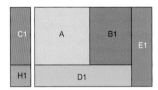

Figure 2

6

5. Sew G1 to F1; press seam toward F1. Sew this unit to the previously pieced unit to complete one Geometric Jazz 1 block referring to Figure 3; press seams toward the G1-F1 unit.

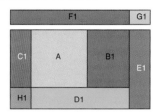

Figure 3

6. Repeat steps 1–5 to complete a total of four Geometric Jazz 1 blocks.

7. Repeat steps 1–5 with A and the B2–H2 pieces to complete a total of four Geometric Jazz 2 blocks referring to Figure 4.

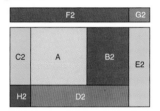

Figure 4

Completing the Bed Runner

1. Select one each Geometric Jazz 1 and Geometric Jazz 2 block and one I strip; join to make an I row as shown in Figure 5. Press seams toward I. Repeat to make a second I row.

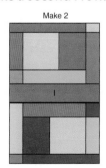

Make 2

Figure 5

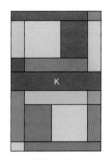

Figure 6

2. Select one each Geometric Jazz 1 and Geometric Jazz 2 block and one K strip; join to make a K row as shown in Figure 6. Press seams toward K.

3. Join two L strips with an M square to make a sashing strip referring to Figure 7; press seams toward L.

Figure 7

4. Repeat step 3 with two J strips and an M square referring to Figure 8.

Figure 8

5. Join the I and K rows with the sashing strips referring to the Placement Diagram for positioning of rows and sashing strips; press seams toward the sashing strips.

6. Sandwich the batting rectangle between the completed runner top and the prepared backing piece; pin or baste layers together to hold. Quilt as desired by hand or machine. *Note: The sample was quilted in parallel lines ½" apart in each strip or rectangle.*

7. When quilting is complete, trim batting and backing fabric even with raw edges of the runner top.

8. Join binding strips on short ends with diagonal seams to make one long strip as shown in Figure 9; trim seams to ¼" and press seams open.

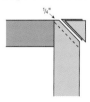

Figure 9

House of White Birches, Berne, Indiana 46711 Clotilde.com

9. Fold the binding strip with wrong sides together along length; press.

10. Sew binding to the runner edges, mitering corners and overlapping ends. Fold binding to the back side and stitch in place to finish the bed runner.

Completing the Shams

1. Select the remaining Geometric Jazz 1 block, one K strip and two each N1 and O1 strips.

2. Sew the K strip to the D1 side of the pieced block; press seam toward K referring to the Geometric Jazz 1 Sham Placement Diagram.

3. Sew an N1 strip to both short ends of the pieced block; press seams toward N1 strips.

4. Sew the O1 strips to the top and bottom of the pieced block to complete the sham top; press seams toward O1 strips.

5. Sandwich a 35" x 28" batting rectangle between the pieced top and one 35" x 28" muslin backing rectangle.

6. Repeat steps 6 and 7 of Completing the Bed Runner to quilt the sham top.

7. Turn under one 21" edge of a sham 17" x 21" back rectangle ¼" and press. Turn under ½" and press again; stitch to hem edge. Repeat with a second back rectangle.

8. Place the two hemmed sham back rectangles right sides together with the quilted sham top with hemmed edges toward the center and overlapping as shown in Figure 10. Pin-baste edges together. Stitch all around edges.

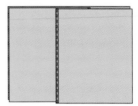

Figure 10

9. Trim corners and turn right side out through center opening; press edges flat to finish.

10. Repeat steps 1–9 with the remaining Geometric Jazz 2 block, I strip and two each N2 and O2 strips to make a second pillow sham referring to the Placement Diagram for positioning of strips. ∎

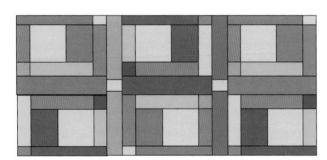

Geometric Jazz Bed Runner
Placement Diagram
67" x 30"

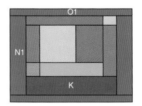

Geometric Jazz 1 Sham
Placement Diagram
27" x 20½"

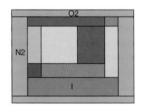

Geometric Jazz 2 Sham
Placement Diagram
27" x 20½"

Tulip Twist
Bed Runner & Shams

Designs by Holly Daniels

These fresh, crisp batiks will bring a touch of spring to any bedroom.

Project Specifications

Skill Level: Confident Beginner
Bed Runner Size: 80½" x 29½"
Sham Size: 26¾" x 20¾" (make 2)
Block Size: 9" x 9"
Number of Blocks: 19

Materials

- 28 assorted 4" x 10" rectangles pastel-color batiks
- ⅜ yard yellow tonal
- 1⅞ yards pink batik
- 3⅛ yards white solid
- 3½ yards green batik
- Backing 89" x 38"
- Batting: 89" x 38" (runner), (2) 35" x 29" (shams)
- Neutral-color all-purpose thread
- Quilting thread
- Template material
- 6 yards ⅜" (9mm) cord
- Basic sewing tools and supplies

Cutting

1. Prepare templates for A and B using patterns given; cut as directed on each piece.

2. Cut one 1½" D square to match each A piece to total 28 D squares.

3. Cut one 2¾" square to match each A piece to total 28 squares. Cut each square in half on one diagonal to make 56 C triangles.

4. Cut two 2½" by fabric width strips white solid; subcut strips into (28) 1½" x 2½" F strips and (14) 2½" squares. Cut each square in half on one diagonal to make a total of 28 E triangles. Cut each F strip at a 45-degree angle on one end to make F pieces as shown in Figure 1.

45-degree angle

Figure 1

5. Cut five 3⅛" by fabric width strips white solid; subcut strips into (56) 3⅛" G squares.

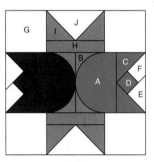

Tulip
9" x 9" Block
Make 14

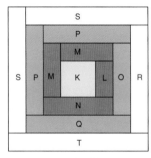

Log Cabin
9" x 9" Block
Make 5

6. Cut one 5" by fabric width strip white solid; subcut strip into seven 5" squares. Cut each square on both diagonals to make 28 J triangles.

7. Cut (13) 1⅝" by fabric width strips white solid; subcut strips into the following: five 1⅝" x 7¼" R; (10) 1⅝" x 8⅜" S; five 1⅝" x 9½" T; and 12 each 1⅝" x 8¾" AA, 1⅝" x 9⅞" BB and 1⅝" x 10¼" FF.

8. Cut two 35" x 29" sham-top backing rectangles white solid.

9. Cut one 3⅛" by fabric width strip yellow tonal; subcut strip into six 3⅛" squares. Cut each square in half on one diagonal to make 12 V triangles. Trim the remainder of the strip to 2¾" and cut five 2¾" K squares.

10. Cut one 3½" by fabric width strip yellow tonal; subcut strip into three 3½" squares. Cut each square on both diagonals to make 12 CC triangles.

11. Cut two 1½" by fabric width strips yellow tonal; subcut strips into four 1½" x 13¼" II strips.

12. Cut one 4¼" by fabric width strip green batik; subcut strip into (28) 1¼" x 4¼" H strips.

13. Cut two 2¾" by fabric width strips green batik; subcut strips into (28) 2¾" squares. Cut each square in half on one diagonal to make 56 I triangles.

14. Cut seven 1⅝" by fabric width strips green batik; subcut strips into the following: five 1⅝" x 2¾" L; (10) 1⅝" x 3⅞" M; five 1⅝" x 5" N; (12) 1⅝" x 4¼" W, (12) 1⅝" x 5⅜" X; and (12) 1⅝" x 5¾" DD.

15. Cut six 2½" by fabric width strips green batik; trim two of the strips to make two 2½" x 30" UU strips. Set aside remaining strips for U borders.

16. Cut two 1½" by fabric width strips green batik; subcut strips into four 1½" x 13¼" II strips.

17. Cut four 4½" by fabric width strips green batik; subcut into four each 4½" x 19¼" GG strips and 4½" x 21¼" HH strips. *Note: Cut one each GG and HH from each strip.*

18. Cut two 21¼" by fabric width strips green batik; subcut strips into four 17½" x 21¼" sham backs.

19. Cut (11) 1⅝" by fabric width strips pink batik; subcut strips into five 1⅝" x 5" O; (10) 1⅝" x 6⅛" P; five 1⅝" x 7¼" Q; (12) 1⅝" x 6½" Y; (12) 1⅝" x 7⅝" Z; and (12) 1⅝" x 8" EE.

20. Cut two 1½" by fabric width strips pink batik; subcut strips into four 1½" x 13¼" II strips.

21. Cut six 2½" by fabric width strips pink batik for bed runner binding.

22. Cut 1½"-wide bias strips pink batik to total 216" or 6 yards for sham piping.

Completing the Tulip Blocks

1. To complete one Tulip block, select two each E, F, H and J pieces and four each B, G and I pieces. Select two sets of matching pieces as follows for each set: one A, one D and two C.

2. Sew an I triangle to each short side of J and add H to complete a green side unit as shown in Figure 2; press seams toward I. Repeat to make a second green side unit.

Make 2

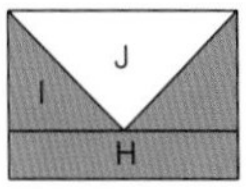

Figure 2

3. Add G to opposite sides of each green side unit to complete the top and bottom rows as shown in Figure 3; press seams toward G.

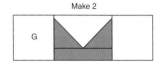

Make 2

Figure 3

4. Mark the center of the curved side of each A piece.

5. Join two B pieces on the short ends as shown in Figure 4; press seam open.

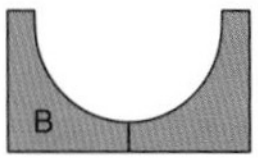

Figure 4

6. Center and sew an A piece to the stitched B unit with the B unit on top when stitching as shown in Figure 5; clip curves and press with seam toward B to complete an A-B unit as shown in Figure 6.

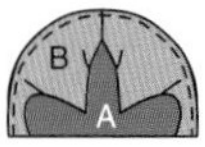

Figure 5

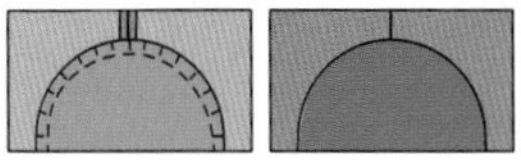

Figure 6

7. Select a D square and two C triangles to match A. Sew F to D and add E to make a D-E-F unit as shown in Figure 7; press seams toward D.

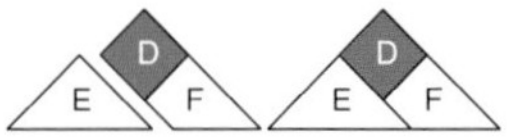

Figure 7

8. Sew a C triangle to each D side of the D-E-F unit to complete a C-D-E-F unit as shown in Figure 8; press seams toward C.

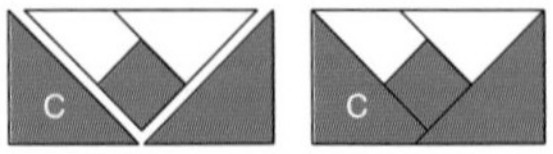

Figure 8

9. Sew the C-D-E-F unit to the A-B unit to complete a tulip unit as shown in Figure 9; press seams toward the A-B unit.

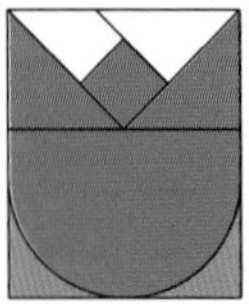

Figure 9

10. Repeat steps 5–9 to complete a second tulip unit.

11. Join the two tulip units to complete the center row as shown in Figure 10; press seam open.

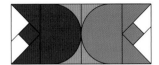

Figure 10

12. Sew the center row between the previously pieced top and bottom rows to complete one Tulip block referring to Figure 11; press seams toward the center row.

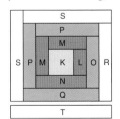

Figure 11

13. Repeat steps 1–12 to complete a total of 14 Tulip blocks.

Completing the Log Cabin Blocks

1. To complete one Log Cabin block, select one each K, L, N, O, Q, R and T strips and two each M, P and S strips.

2. Sew L to K; press seam toward L. Add M as shown in Figure 12; press seam toward M.

Figure 12

3. Continue to add strips around the stitched unit to complete one Log Cabin block as shown in Figure 13, pressing seams toward the mostly recently added strip before adding the next strip.

Figure 13

4. Repeat steps 1–3 to complete a total of five Log Cabin blocks.

Completing the Side Triangle Units

1. To complete one side triangle Log Cabiln unit, select one each V, W, X, Y, Z, AA and BB. Sew W to V, with W extending on one end as shown in Figure 14; press seam toward W.

Figure 14

2. Sew X to the V-W unit as shown in Figure 15; press seam toward X.

Figure 15

3. Continue to add the Y, Z, AA and BB strips to the pieced unit as shown in Figure 16; press seams toward the most recently added strip before adding the next strip.

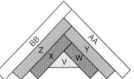

Figure 16

4. Trim excess pieces even with the V triangle using a straightedge as shown in Figure 17.

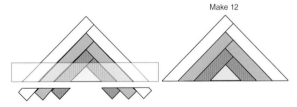

Figure 17

5. Repeat steps 1–4 to complete a total of 12 side triangle Log Cabin units.

Completing the Corner Units

1. Center and sew a DD, EE and FF strip to the long edge of a CC triangle as shown in Figure 18; press seams away from CC.

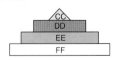

Figure 18

14

2. Place the straightedge even with the edge of CC and to the bottom end of FF and trim the angle as shown in Figure 19; repeat on the opposite side to complete a corner unit.

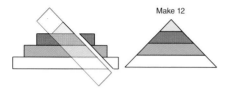

Make 12

Figure 19

3. Repeat steps 1 and 2 to complete a total of 12 corner units.

Completing the Bed Runner

1. Sew a Log Cabin block between two Tulip blocks and add a side triangle unit to each end to make an XX row as shown in Figure 20; press seams away from the Tulip blocks. Repeat to make three XX rows.

XX Row
Make 3

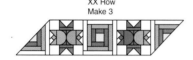

Figure 20

2. Sew a Log Cabin block between two Tulip blocks and add one side triangle unit and one corner unit to complete a YY row as shown in Figure 21; press seams away from the Tulip blocks. Repeat to make a second YY row.

YY Row
Make 2

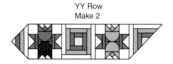

Figure 21

3. Sew a side triangle unit to opposite sides of a Tulip block and add a corner unit to complete one end row as shown in Figure 22; press seams away from the Tulip block. Repeat to make a second end row.

End Row
Make 2

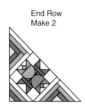

Figure 22

4. Arrange and join the XX, YY and end rows to complete the pieced center referring to Figure 23; press seams in one direction.

Figure 23

5. Join the U strips on the short ends to make a long strip; press seams open. Subcut strip into two 77" U strips.

6. Sew the U strips to opposite long sides of the pieced center; press seams toward U strips.

7. Sew an UU strip to opposite ends of the pieced center to complete the runner top; press seams toward the UU strips.

8. Sandwich the 89" x 38" piece of batting between the completed runner top and the 89" x 38" prepared backing piece; pin or baste layers together to hold. Quilt as desired by hand or machine.

9. When quilting is complete, trim batting and backing fabric even with raw edges of the runner top.

10. Join binding strips on short ends with diagonal seams to make one long strip as shown in Figure 24; trim seams to ¼" and press seams open.

¼"

Figure 24

11. Fold the binding strip with wrong sides together along length; press.

12. Sew binding to the runner edges, mitering corners and overlapping ends. Fold binding to the back side and stitch in place to finish the bed runner.

Completing the Shams

1. To complete one sham, sew a corner unit to each side of a Tulip block as shown in Figure 25; press seams toward corner units.

Figure 25

2. Sew a yellow II to a green II to a pink II to make an II unit; press seams away from the yellow strip. Repeat to make a second II unit.

3. Sew an II unit to opposite sides of the framed Tulip block to complete the pieced center as shown in Figure 26; press seams toward II units.

Figure 26

4. Sew GG strips to the top and bottom, and HH strips to the ends of the pieced center referring to the Placement Diagram to complete one sham top; press seams toward GG and HH strips.

5. Repeat steps 1–4 to complete a second sham top.

6. Sandwich the 35" x 29" batting rectangle between one white solid 35" x 29" backing rectangle; pin and baste to hold.

7. Quilt as desired by hand or machine; trim excess batting and backing even with the pieced top.

8. Repeat steps 6 and 7 with the second pieced top, batting and white backing pieces.

9. Join the previously cut pink batik 1½"-wide bias strips on the short ends to make a long strip; press seams open.

10. Fold the bias strip over the cord right side out; stitch close to cord to create piping.

11. Pin and baste piping in place on the top side of the sham, easing around corners as shown in Figure 27. Repeat on second sham.

Figure 27

12. Turn under one 21¼" edge of each green batik back ¼" and press. Turn under ½" press and stitch to hem.

13. Layer two hemmed back rectangles right sides together with a quilted sham top, matching the unhemmed edges and overlapping the hemmed edges as shown in Figure 28; stitch all around.

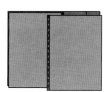

Figure 28

14. Turn right side out through the opening to finish. Insert bed pillow through opening.

15. Repeat steps 9–14 to complete the second sham.

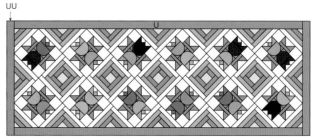

Tulip Twist Bed Runner
Placement Diagram
80½" x 29½"

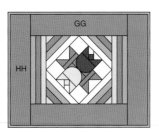

Tulip Twist Sham
Placement Diagram
26¾" x 20¾"

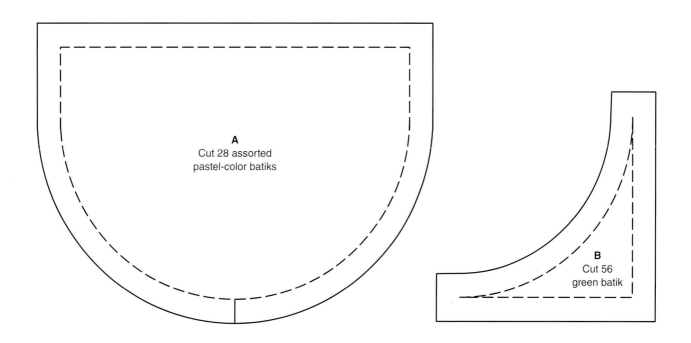

A
Cut 28 assorted
pastel-color batiks

B
Cut 56
green batik

Pineapple Pleasures

Design by Nancy McNally

Black and white with a touch of lime will spruce up any bed.

Project Specifications
Skill Level: Confident Beginner
Bed Runner Size: 83" x 27"
Block Size: 14" x 14"
Number of Blocks: 5

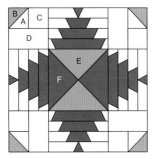

Pineapple
14" x 14" Block
Make 5

Materials
- ½ yard lime green tonal
- 1⅛ yards black solid
- 1⅛ yards white solid
- Backing 91" x 35"
- Batting 91" x 35"
- White all-purpose thread
- Quilting thread
- Basic sewing tools and supplies

Cutting
1. Cut one 2⅞" by fabric width strip white solid; subcut strip into (10) 2⅞" A squares.

2. Cut two 2½" by fabric width strips white solid; subcut strips into (20) 2½" C squares.

3. Cut two 4½" by fabric width strips white solid; subcut strips into (20) 2½" x 4½" D rectangles.

4. Cut two 6½" by fabric width strips white solid; subcut strips into (20) 4" x 6½" G rectangles. *Note: If using the templates provided instead of the no-template method, prepare a template for G. Place the two strips with right sides together and cut as*

directed on pattern and as shown in Figure 1 to cut G and GR pieces at the same time.

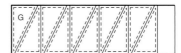

Figure 1

5. Cut four 7" by fabric width strips white solid; set aside three strips for K. Subcut the remaining strip into two 7" x 14½" L strips.

6. Cut one 7¾" by fabric width strip lime green tonal; subcut strip into two 7¾" I squares. Cut each square on both diagonals to make a total of eight I triangles. Trim the remaining strip to 7¼" and cut three 7¼" E squares. Cut each square on both diagonals to make a total of 12 E triangles. Set aside two E triangles for another project.

7. Cut one 2⅞" by fabric width strip lime green tonal; subcut strip into (10) 2⅞" B squares.

8. Cut four 6⅞" by fabric width strips black solid; subcut strips into (20) 6½" x 6⅞" H rectangles. *Note: If using the template method, cut strips 6½" by fabric width, prepare a template for H and use the template to cut 20 H triangles from the strips.*

9. Cut one 7¾" by fabric width strip black solid; subcut strip into two 7¾" J squares. Cut each square on both diagonals to make a total of eight J triangles. Trim the strip to 7¼" and cut three 7¼" F squares. Cut each square on both diagonals to make a total of 12 F triangles. Set aside two F triangles for another project.

10. Cut six 2¼" by fabric width strips black solid for binding.

Completing the Block Corner Units
1. Mark a diagonal line from corner to corner on the wrong side of each A square.

2. Place an A square right sides together with a B square; stitch ¼" on each side of the marked line. Cut apart on the marked line and press open with seam toward B to complete two A-B units as shown in Figure 2. Repeat with the remaining A and B squares to complete a total of 20 A-B units.

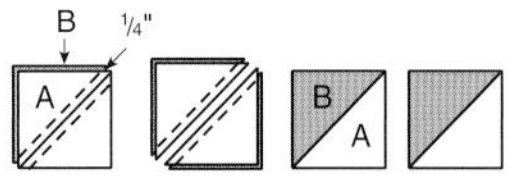

Figure 2

3. Sew an A-B unit to a C square and add D to complete a corner unit as shown in Figure 3; press seam toward C and then D. Repeat to complete a total of 20 corner units. Set aside.

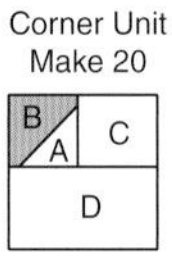

Corner Unit
Make 20

Figure 3

Completing the Block Side Units

Note: If G, GR and H pieces were cut using templates, skip to step 4.

1. Select one each G rectangle; mark a line ⅜" in from the bottom left corner and from the top right corner as shown in Figure 4. Place a rotary ruler on each mark and cut to make two G triangles, again referring to Figure 4. Repeat with nine more G rectangles to make a total of 20 G pieces.

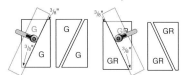

Figure 4

2. Repeat step 1 with the remaining G pieces except mark the lines ⅜" from the lower right corner and ⅜" in from the upper left corner to make a total of 20 GR pieces, again referring to Figure 4.

3. Fold each H rectangle on the 6½" side and crease to mark the center. Place a straightedge on one bottom corner, align with center crease and trim as shown in Figure 5; repeat on the opposite bottom corner to make the H triangle, again referring to Figure 5. Repeat on each H rectangle.

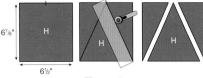

Figure 5

4. Select one each G, GR and H triangle. Sew the G and GR triangles to H to make a G-H unit as shown in Figure 6; press seams toward G and GR. Repeat to make a total of 20 G-H units.

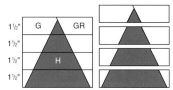

Make 20

Figure 6

5. Cut a G-H unit apart into 1½" units as shown in Figure 7.

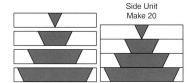

Figure 7

6. Rearrange the units and stitch together to make a side unit as shown in Figure 8; press seams in one direction. *Note: The stitched unit should now measure 6½" x 4½".*

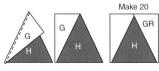

Side Unit
Make 20

Figure 8

7. Repeat steps 5 and 6 to complete a total of 20 side units.

Completing the Blocks

1. Sew an E triangle to an F triangle as shown in Figure 9; press seam toward F. Repeat to make 10 E-F units.

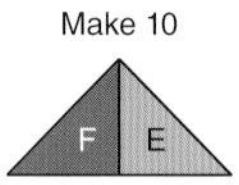

Make 10

Figure 9

2. Join two E-F units to make a center unit as shown in Figure 10; press seam to one side. Repeat to make a total of five center units.

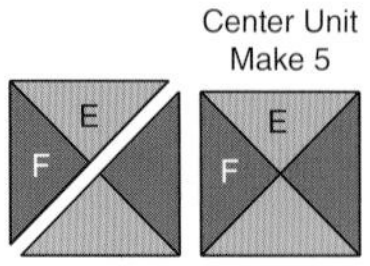

Center Unit
Make 5

Figure 10

3. To complete one Pineapple block, select one center unit and four each side and corner units.

4. Sew a side unit to opposite sides of the center unit to complete the center row as shown in Figure 11; press seams toward the center unit.

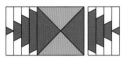

Figure 11

5. Sew a corner unit to opposite sides of a side unit to complete the top row as shown in Figure 12; press seams toward the corner unit. Repeat to make the bottom row.

Figure 12

6. Sew the center row between the top and bottom rows to complete one Pineapple block as shown in Figure 13; press seams away from the center row.

Figure 13

7. Repeat steps 3–6 to complete a total of five Pineapple blocks.

Completing the Bed Runner

1. Join the five Pineapple blocks to complete the pieced center; press seams open.

2. Join the K strips on short ends to make a long strip; press seams open. Subcut strip into two 70½" K strips.

3. Sew a K strip to opposite long sides of the pieced center; press seams toward K strips.

4. Sew an I triangle to a J triangle as shown in Figure 14; press seam toward J. Repeat with remaining I and J triangles to make eight I-J units.

Figure 14

5. Join two I-J units to make a corner unit, again referring to Figure 14; press seam to one side.

6. Repeat steps 4 and 5 to make a total of four corner units.

7. Sew a corner unit to each end of each L strip to make two end strips as shown in Figure 15; press seams toward L.

Figure 15

8. Sew an end strip to each short end of the pieced center to complete the runner top; press seams toward the end strips.

9. Sandwich the batting rectangle between the completed runner top and the prepared backing piece; pin or baste layers together to hold. Quilt as desired by hand or machine. ***Note:*** *The sample was quilted in a swirl pattern in the blocks, a feather pattern in the borders and petal shapes within the corner square triangles.*

10. When quilting is complete, trim batting and backing fabric even with raw edges of the runner top.

11. Join binding strips on short ends with diagonal seams to make one long strip as shown in Figure 16; trim seams to ¼" and press seams open.

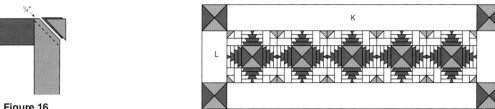

Figure 16

12. Fold the binding strip with wrong sides together along length; press.

13. Sew binding to the runner top edges, mitering corners and overlapping ends. Fold binding to the back side and stitch in place to finish the bed runner. ▮

Pineapple Pleasures
Placement Diagram
83" x 27"

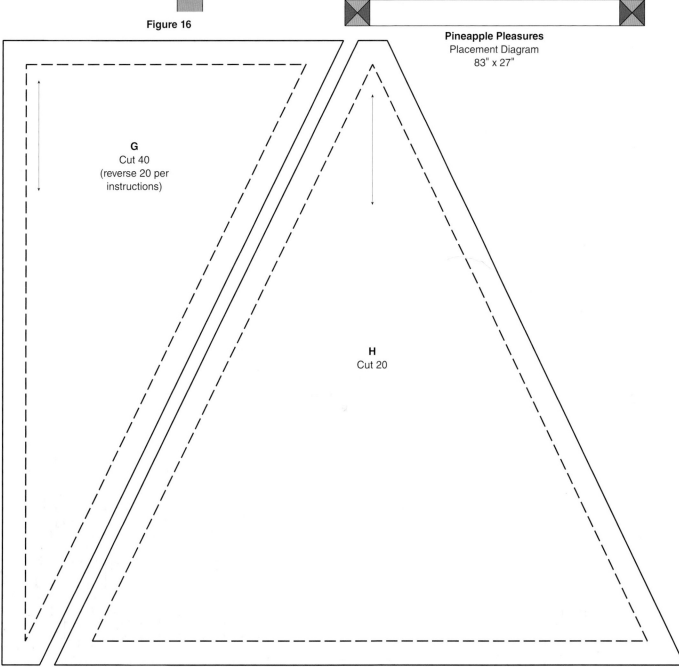

G
Cut 40
(reverse 20 per
instructions)

H
Cut 20

Summer Blossoms

Designs by Phyllis Dobbs

Take an ordinary bedroom and make it spectacular with bright and funky bed accents. This bed runner and the matching shams will add a spark of excitement to any room.

Bed Runner

Project Specifications
Skill Level: Beginner
Bed Runner Size: 81" x 27"
Block Size: 18" x 18"
Number of Blocks: 4

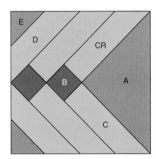

Large Summer Blossoms
18" x 18" Block
Make 4

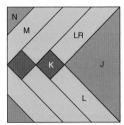

Small Summer Blossoms
11" x 11" Block
Make 4

Materials
- ⅜ yard fuchsia tonal
- ½ yard coordinating stripe
- ⅔ yard black paisley
- ⅔ yard green floral print
- 1⅜ yards gold tonal
- ⅞ yards gold floral print
- Backing 89" x 35"
- Batting 89" x 35"

- All-purpose thread to match fabrics
- Multicolored quilting thread
- ½ yard 18"-wide fusible web
- Basic sewing tools and supplies

Cutting

1. Cut one 19¼" by fabric width strip green floral print; subcut the strip into one 19¼" square. Cut the square on both diagonals to make four A triangles.

2. Trim the remainder of the strip cut in step 1 to 5⅜" and subcut the strip into four 5⅜" squares. Cut each square in half on one diagonal to make eight E triangles.

3. Cut one 3⅝" by fabric width strip black paisley; subcut strip into eight 3⅝" B squares.

4. Cut six 2½" by fabric width strips black paisley for binding.

5. Cut one 13⅞" by fabric width strip gold tonal; subcut strip into eight 3⅝" x 13⅞" strips. Cut each end of the strip at a 45-degree angle to make eight D strips as shown in Figure 1.

Figure 1

6. Cut two 13⅝" by fabric width strips gold tonal. Subcut these strips into (16) 3⅝" x 13⅝" strips. Cut a 45-degree angle off the left end of eight strips for C and off the right end of the remaining strips for CR as shown in Figure 2.

Figure 2

House of White Birches, Berne, Indiana 46711   Clotilde.com

26

7. Cut four 2½" by fabric width F strips coordinating stripe.

8. Cut two 2½" x 22½" G strips coordinating stripe. *Note: The sample has the stripe strips cut along the length of the stripe; yardage has not been included for this option.*

9. Cut four 3" by fabric width H strips gold floral print.

10. Cut two 3" x 27½" I strips gold floral print.

11. Trace the large flower and large flower center onto the paper side of the fusible web as directed on patterns for number to cut, leaving ½" between pieces when tracing.

12. Cut out shapes leaving a margin around each one. Fuse shapes to the wrong side of fabrics as directed on patterns; cut out shapes on traced lines. Remove paper backing.

Completing the Blocks

1. To complete one Large Summer Blossoms block, sew C to A as shown in Figure 3; press seam toward C.

Figure 3

2. Sew CR to B and sew to the A-C unit as shown in Figure 4; press seam toward the B-CR unit.

Figure 4

4. Repeat steps 1 and 2 to add a second set of B, C and CR pieces as shown in Figure 5.

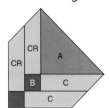

Figure 5

5. Sew D strips to the pieced unit and add E triangles to the D sides to complete one Large Summer Blossoms block as shown in Figure 6; press seams toward D and then E.

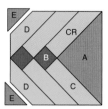

Figure 6

6. Repeat Steps 1–5 to complete a total of four Large Summer Blossoms blocks.

Completing the Bed Runner

1. Join the four Large Summer Blossoms blocks to complete the pieced center as shown in Figure 7; press seams to one side.

Figure 7

2. Center and fuse a large flower on the seams joining the blocks referring to Figure 8; center and fuse the large flower center on the flower.

Figure 8

3. Using thread to match the appliqué shapes, machine-stitch the shapes in place using a close, narrow zigzag stitch.

4. Join the F strips on short ends to make one long strip, press seams open; subcut the strip into two 72½" F strips.

5. Sew the F strips to opposite long sides and G strips to the short ends of the pieced center; press seams toward F and G strips.

6. Join the H strips on short ends to make a long strip; press seams open. Subcut strip into two 76½" H strips.

7. Sew the H strips to opposite long sides and I strips to the short ends of the pieced center to complete the pieced top; press seams toward H and I strips.

8. Sandwich the batting rectangle between the completed runner top and the prepared backing piece; pin or baste layers together to hold. Mark quilting design and quilt as desired by hand or machine.

9. When quilting is complete, remove pins or basting. Trim batting and backing fabric even with raw edges of the runner top.

10. Join binding strips on short ends with diagonal seams to make one long strip as shown in Figure 9; trim seams to ¼" and press seams open.

Figure 9

11. Fold the binding strip with wrong sides together along length; press.

12. Sew binding to the runner matching raw edges, mitering corners and overlapping ends. Fold binding to the back side and stitch in place to finish the bed runner.

Shams

Project Specifications
Skill Level: Beginner
Sham Size: 28" x 19"
Block Size: 11" x 11"
Number of Blocks: 4 (2 shams)

Materials
- 1 fat quarter fuchsia tonal
- ⅛ yard black paisley
- ½ yard coordinating stripe
- ⅝ yard gold tonal
- ¾ yard gold floral print
- 1⅔ yards green floral print
- 1¾ yards muslin
- Batting: (2) 36" x 27" rectangles
- All-purpose thread to match fabrics
- Multicolored quilting thread
- ½ yard 18"-wide fusible web
- Basic sewing tools and supplies

Cutting
1. Cut two rectangles muslin 36" x 27" for sham quilt-top backing.

2. Cut two 19½" by fabric width strips green floral print; subcut strips into four 17½" x 19½" back rectangles.

3. Cut one 12¼" by fabric width strip green floral print; subcut strip into one 12¼" square. Cut the square on both diagonals to make four J triangles.

4. Cut one 2½" by fabric width strip black paisley; subcut strip into eight 2½" K squares.

5. Cut one 9" by fabric width strip gold tonal; subcut strip into eight 2½" x 9" strips. Cut each end of the strip at a 45-degree angle to make eight M strips as shown in Figure 10.

Figure 10

6. Cut one 8⅝" by fabric width strip gold tonal; subcut strip into (16) 2½" x 8⅝" strips. Cut a 45-degree angle off the left end of eight strips for L and off the right end of the remaining strips for LR as shown in Figure 11.

Figure 11

7. Cut four 2" x 22½" O strips and four 2" x 14½" P strips coordinating stripe. ***Note:*** *The sample has the stripe strips cut along the length of the stripe; yardage has not been included for this option.*

8. Cut four 3" x 25½" Q strips and four 2¼" x 19½" R strips gold floral print.

9. Trace the small flower and small flower center onto the paper side of the fusible web as directed on patterns for number to cut, leaving ½" between pieces when tracing.

10. Cut out shapes leaving a margin around each one. Fuse shapes to the wrong side of fabrics as directed on patterns; cut out shapes on traced lines. Remove paper backing.

Completing the Blocks
1. To complete one Small Summer Blossoms block, sew L to J as shown in Figure 12; press seam toward L.

Figure 12

2. Sew LR to K and sew to the J-L unit as shown in Figure 13; press seam toward the K-LR unit.

Figure 13

4. Repeat steps 1 and 2 to add a second set of K, L and LR pieces as shown in Figure 14.

Figure 14

5. Sew an M strip to the pieced unit and add N to the M sides to complete one Small Summer Blossoms block as shown in Figure 15; press seams toward M and then N.

Figure 15

6. Repeat Steps 1–5 to complete a total of four Small Summer Blossoms blocks.

Completing the Shams

1. Join two Small Summer Blossoms blocks to complete one sham top.

2. Appliqué a small flower motif to the center of the sham top as in steps 2 and 3 of Completing the Bed Runner.

3. Sew an O strip to opposite long sides and P strips to the short ends of the sham top; press seams toward O and P strips.

4. Sew a Q strip to opposite long sides and R strips to the short ends of the sham top; press seams toward Q and R strips.

5. Sandwich the batting rectangle between the completed sham top and a muslin sham quilt top backing rectangle; pin or baste layers together to hold. Quilt as desired by hand or machine.

6. When quilting is complete, trim batting and muslin even with raw edges of the sham top.

7. Repeat steps 1–6 to complete a second sham top.

8. Turn under one 19½" edge of each green floral print 17½" x 19½" back rectangle ¼" and press. Turn under ½"; press and stitch to hem.

9. Layer two hemmed back rectangles right sides together with a quilted sham top, matching the unhemmed edges and overlapping the hemmed edges as shown in Figure 16; stitch all around.

Figure 16

10. Turn right side out through the opening to finish. Insert bed pillow through opening.

11. Repeat steps 9 and 10 to complete the second sham. ∎

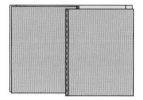

Summer Blossoms Sham
Placement Diagram
28" x 19"

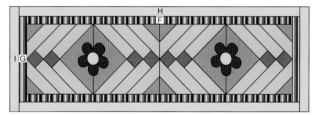

Summer Blossoms Bed Runner
Placement Diagram
81" x 27"

Large Flower
Cut 2 fuchsia tonal

Large Flower Center
Cut 2 gold floral print

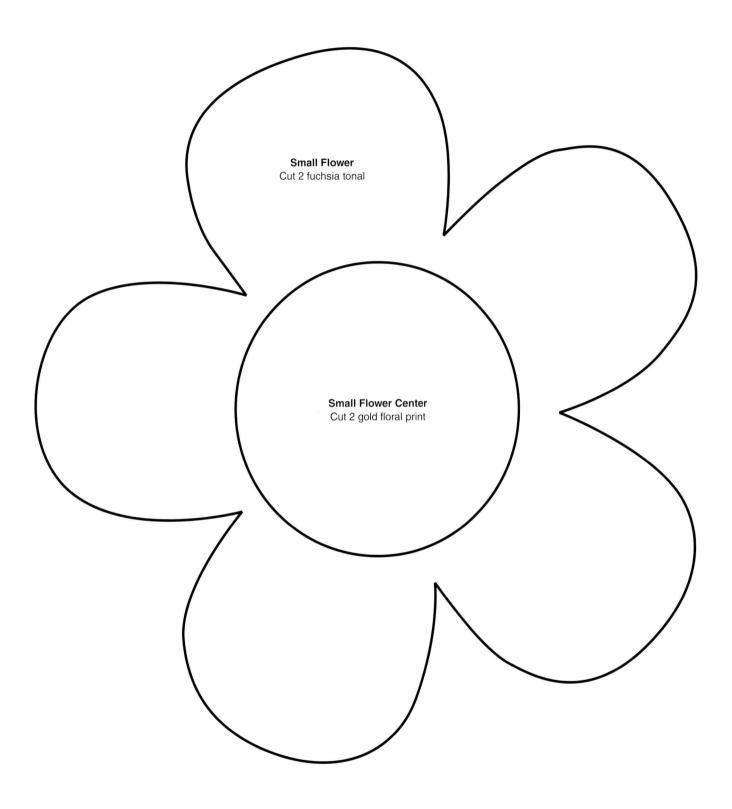

Small Flower
Cut 2 fuchsia tonal

Small Flower Center
Cut 2 gold floral print

House of White Birches, Berne, Indiana 46711   Clotilde.com

Celebration

Designs by Carol Zentgraf

If an American or patriotic theme is what you're looking for, here it is—or maybe you just like star patterns. It's easy to change the colors to make this set your own way.

Project Specifications
Skill Level: Advanced
Bed Runner Size: 73½" x 24"
Sham Size: 28" x 21½"
Block Size: 11" x 11"
Number of Blocks: 14

Celebration Star
11" x 11" Block
Make 14

Materials
• ¼ yard navy-with-white large dots
• ½ yard navy-with-white small dots
• ½ yard red-with-white large dots
• ⅝ yard navy solid
• ⅝ yard red star print
• ⅝ yard red-with-white small dots
• ⅔ yard red solid
• 1½ yards white solid
• 2¾ yards navy star print
• Backing 82" x 32"
• Batting 82" x 32"
• Neutral-color all-purpose thread
• Quilting thread
• Ruler with 45-degree-angle mark
• Basic sewing tools and supplies

Cutting
1. Cut (12) 1¼" by fabric width strips each red star print (A) and red-with-white small dots (F).

2. Cut four 1¼" by fabric width strips each navy-with-white small dots (D) and navy star print (G).

3. Cut eight 1¼" by fabric width strips white solid (C).

4. Cut six 3¾" by fabric width strips white solid; subcut strips into (56) 3¾" H squares.

5. Cut two 5¾" by fabric width strips white solid; subcut strips into (14) 5¾" squares. Cut each square on both diagonals to make 56 I triangles.

6. Cut (14) 1¼" by fabric width B strips navy solid.

7. Cut (15) 1¼" by fabric width E strips red solid.

8. Cut two 1¼" x 22½" J strips red-with-white small dots.

9. Cut two 22" by fabric width strips navy star print; subcut strips into four 16" x 22" sham back pieces.

10. Cut four 1½" x 22½" K strips navy star print.

11. Cut four 5½" by fabric width strips navy star print; subcut strips into four 5½" x 15" T strips

12. Cut four 3" x 28½" U strips navy star print.

13. Cut five 2¼" by fabric width strips navy star print for binding.

14. Cut two 1½" x 22½" L strips navy-with-white large dots.

15. Cut four 1½" by fabric width M strips navy-with-white large dots.

16. Cut five 1¼" by fabric width strips navy-with-white small dots; subcut strips into two 1¼" x 11½" N strips, four 1¼" x 13¼" P strips and six 1¼" x 15" R strips.

17. Cut nine 1½" by fabric width strips red-with-white large dots; subcut strips into two 1½" x 11½" O strips, four 1½" x 13¼" Q strips, six 1½" x 15" S strips and four 1½" x 28½" V strips.

34

Completing the Blocks

1. Sew an A strip to a B strip to a C strip with right sides together along length to make an A-B-C strip set; press seams toward A. Repeat to make a second strip.

2. Trim one end of the strip at a 45-degree angle as shown in Figure 1.

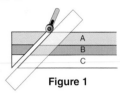

Figure 1

3. Subcut the trimmed strip into (28) 1¼" A-B-C segments as shown in Figure 2.

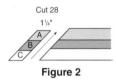

Figure 2

4. Repeat steps 1 and 2 to make two strip sets each in the following combinations: A-B-D, A-E-E, E-D-C, F-F-F, F-B-C, F-B-G, F-E-E, E-G-C and A-A-A. *Note: Refer ahead to Figure 3 and press in the direction of arrows so that seams are offset when they are joined later.*

5. Repeat steps 1 and 2 to make three E-B-B strip sets. *Note: Refer ahead to Figure 3 and press in the direction of arrows so that seams are offset when they are joined later.*

6. Subcut all strip sets into 1¼" segments referring to Figure 3 for the number of segments needed of each combination.

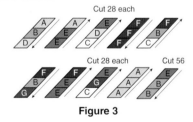

Figure 3

7. Select one each A-B-C, A-B-D and A-E-E unit and join to make an A diamond unit as shown in Figure 4. Repeat to make a total of 28 A diamond units. Press seams in direction of arrow, again referring to Figure 4.

Figure 4

8. Repeat step 7 with E-D-C, E-B-B and F-F-F units to make 28 B diamond units referring to Figure 5. Press seams, again referring to Figure 5.

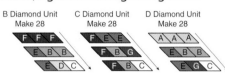

Figure 5

9. Repeat step 7 with F-B-C, F-B-G and F-E-E units to make 28 C diamond units and press seams, again referring to Figure 5.

10. Repeat step 7 with E-G-C, E-B-B and A-A-A units to make 28 D diamond units and press seams, again referring to Figure 5.

11. On the wrong side of diamond units, mark the ¼" seam intersections at the side and C tips of each diamond unit as shown in Figure 6.

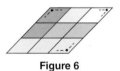

Figure 6

12. To make one Celebration Star block, join one each A, B, C and D diamond unit to make half of the star design, stopping stitching at the ¼" seam intersections as shown in Figure 7; press seams in one direction. Repeat to make the second half of the star design.

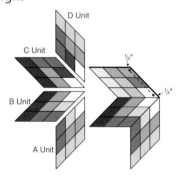

Figure 7

13. Join the two halves of the star design to complete the block center as shown in Figure 8; press seam to one side with the unstitched center parts pressed in a swirling pattern as shown in Figure 8.

Figure 8

14. Sew in the H corner squares starting at the inside and stitching to the outside edge as shown in Figure 9; press seams toward H.

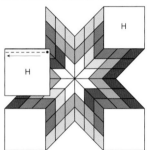

Figure 9

15. Repeat step 14 with the I triangles, pressing seams toward I, to complete one Celebration Star block as shown in Figure 10.

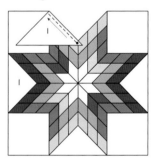

Figure 10

16. Repeat steps 12–15 to complete a total of 14 blocks, pressing seams in half the blocks toward H and I, and half with seams toward the pieced units for ease of joining blocks together later.

Completing the Bed Runner

1. Referring to the Placement Diagram throughout, join two Celebration Star blocks to make a row; press seams open. Repeat to make six two-block rows.

2. Join two two-block rows to make a four-block unit; press seams open. Repeat to make three four-block units.

3. Sew a J strip between two K strips to make a J-K strip; press seams toward K. Repeat to make a second J-K strip.

4. Join the four-block units with the J-K strips to complete the pieced center; press seams toward the J-K strips.

5. Sew an L strip to opposite short ends of the pieced center; press seams toward L strips.

6. Join the M strips on the short ends to make a long strip; press seams open. Subcut strip into two 74" M strips.

7. Sew an M strip to opposite long sides of the pieced center to complete the runner top; press seams toward M strips.

8. Sandwich the batting rectangle between the completed runner top and the prepared backing piece; pin or baste layers together to hold. Quilt as desired by hand or machine.

9. When quilting is complete, trim batting and backing fabric even with raw edges of the runner top.

10. Join binding strips on short ends with diagonal seams to make one long strip as shown in Figure 11; trim seams to ¼" and press seams open.

Figure 11

11. Fold the binding strip with wrong sides together along length; press.

12. Sew binding to the runner top edges, mitering corners and overlapping ends. Fold binding to the back side and stitch in place to finish the bed runner.

Completing the Shams

1. Sew an N strip to an O strip; press seam toward O. Sew the N-O strip to one side of one Celebration Star block as shown in Figure 12; press seams toward the N-O strip.

Figure 12

2. Sew a P strip to a Q strip; press seam toward Q. Repeat to make a second P-Q strip. Sew one strip to the bottom edge and the second strip to the adjacent edge of the pieced unit as shown in Figure 13; press seam toward the P-Q strips.

Figure 13

3. Sew an R strip to an S strip; press seam toward S. Repeat to make three R-S strips. Sew an R-S strip to the top and both ends of the pieced unit as shown in Figure 14; press seams toward R-S strips.

Figure 14

4. Referring to the Placement Diagram, sew T strips to opposite short ends and U strips to opposite long sides of the pieced unit; press seams toward T and U strips. Sew V strips to the U sides of the pieced unit to complete one sham top; press seams toward V strips.

5. Repeat steps 1–4 to complete a second sham top. *Note: The sample shams were not quilted.*

6. Turn under one 22" edge of each navy star print back rectangle ¼" and press. Turn under ½", press again and stitch to hem.

7. Layer two hemmed back rectangles right sides together with a sham top, matching the unhemmed edges and overlapping the hemmed edges as shown in Figure 15; stitch all around.

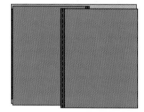

Figure 15

8. Turn right side out through the opening to finish. Insert bed pillow through opening.

9. Repeat steps 6–8 to complete the second sham. ■

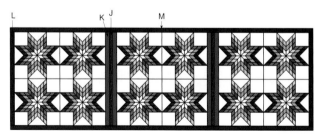

Celebration Bed Runner
Placement Diagram
73½" x 24"

COLOR KEY
- Red star print
- Navy solid
- White solid
- Navy-with-white small dots
- Red solid
- Red-with-white small dots
- Navy star print
- Red-with-white large dots
- Navy-with-white large dots

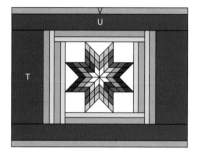

Celebration Sham
Placement Diagram
28" x 21½"

Warm Splendor

Design by Phyllis Dobbs

Bring the splendor of warm autumn colors to your bed with this fast and easy bed runner.

Project Specifications
Skill Level: Confident Beginner
Bed Runner Size: 77½" x 30" with prairie points
Block Size: 20" x 20"
Number of Blocks: 3

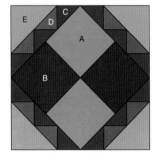

Warm Splendor
20" x 20" Block
Make 3

Materials
- **Note:** *All fabrics have gold metallic in the prints.*
- ⅝ yard vegetable print
- ⅝ yard black with orange and rust leaves
- ⅝ yard rust-with-gold leaves
- ⅞ yard black leaf print
- 1⅛ yards green-with-gold leaves
- Backing 86" x 38"
- Batting 86" x 38"
- All-purpose thread to match fabrics
- Multicolored quilting thread
- Basic sewing tools and supplies

Cutting
1. Cut two 7⅝" by fabric width strips rust-with-gold leaves; subcut strips into six 7⅝" A squares.

2. Cut two 7⅝" by fabric width strips black with orange and rust leaves; subcut strips into six 7⅝" B squares.

3. Cut two 6" by fabric width strips green-with-gold leaves; subcut strips into nine 6" squares. Cut each square on both diagonals to make 36 C triangles.

4. Cut three 2½" by fabric width F strips green-with-gold leaves.

5. Cut two 2½" x 24½" G strips green-with-gold leaves.

6. Cut one 8¾" by fabric width strip green-with-gold leaves; subcut strip into four 8¾" squares. Cut each square on both diagonals to make 16 J triangles.

7. Cut one 6" by fabric width strip black leaf print; subcut strip into six 6" squares. Cut each square on both diagonals to make 24 D triangles.

8. Cut three 3½" by fabric width H strips black leaf print.

9. Cut two 3½" x 30½" I strips black leaf print.

10. Cut two 7½" by fabric width strips vegetable print; subcut strips into six 7½" squares. Cut each square in half on one diagonal to make 12 E triangles.

Completing the Blocks
1. To complete one Warm Splendor block, select two each A and B squares, four E triangles, 12 C triangles and eight D triangles.

2. Sew A to B; press seam toward B. Repeat. Join the two pieced units to complete the block center as shown in Figure 1; press seam to one side.

Figure 1

3. Join two D triangles with three C triangles to make a triangle strip as shown in Figure 2; press seams toward D. Repeat to make a total of four triangle strips.

Make 4

Figure 2

4. Sew an E triangle to the D side of each triangle strip to complete the corner triangles referring to Figure 3; press seams toward E.

Figure 3

5. Sew a corner triangle to each side of the A-B unit to complete one Warm Splendor block referring to Figure 4; press seams toward the A-B unit.

Figure 4

6. Repeat Steps 1–5 to complete a total of three Warm Splendor blocks.

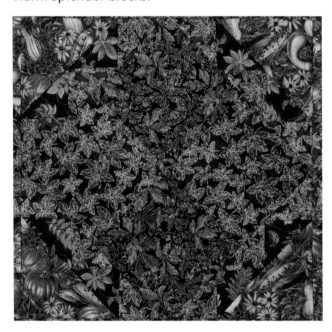

Completing the Bed Runner

1. Join the three Warm Splendor blocks to complete the pieced center; press seams to one side.

2. Join the F strips on short ends to make a long strip; press seams open. Subcut strip into two 60½" F strips.

3. Sew the F strips to opposite long sides and G strips to the short ends of the pieced center; press seams toward F and G strips.

4. Join the H strips on short ends to make a long strip; press seams open. Subcut strip into two 64½" H strips.

5. Sew the H strips to opposite long sides and I strips to the short ends of the pieced center to complete the pieced top; press seams toward H and I strips.

6. Place two J triangles right sides together; stitch on the two short sides, leaving long edge open as shown in Figure 5; trim point at corner. Turn right side out; press flat to complete one J unit. Repeat with all J triangles to make eight J units.

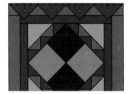

Figure 5

7. Position, pin and baste four J triangle units to each end of the pieced top, overlapping seam allowances referring to Figure 6.

Figure 6

8. Place the batting on a flat surface with the pieced top right side up on top; place the prepared backing piece right sides together with the pieced top. Pin or baste layers together.

9. Stitch all around edges, leaving a 6" opening on one long side. Trim corners.

10. Turn right side out through opening; press edges flat, flipping J units out as shown in Placement Diagram. Press opening edges to the inside; hand-stitch opening closed.

11. Quilt as desired by hand or machine to finish. ■

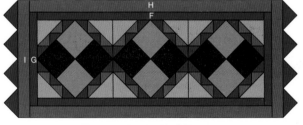

Warm Splendor Bed Runner
Placement Diagram
77½" x 30" with prairie points

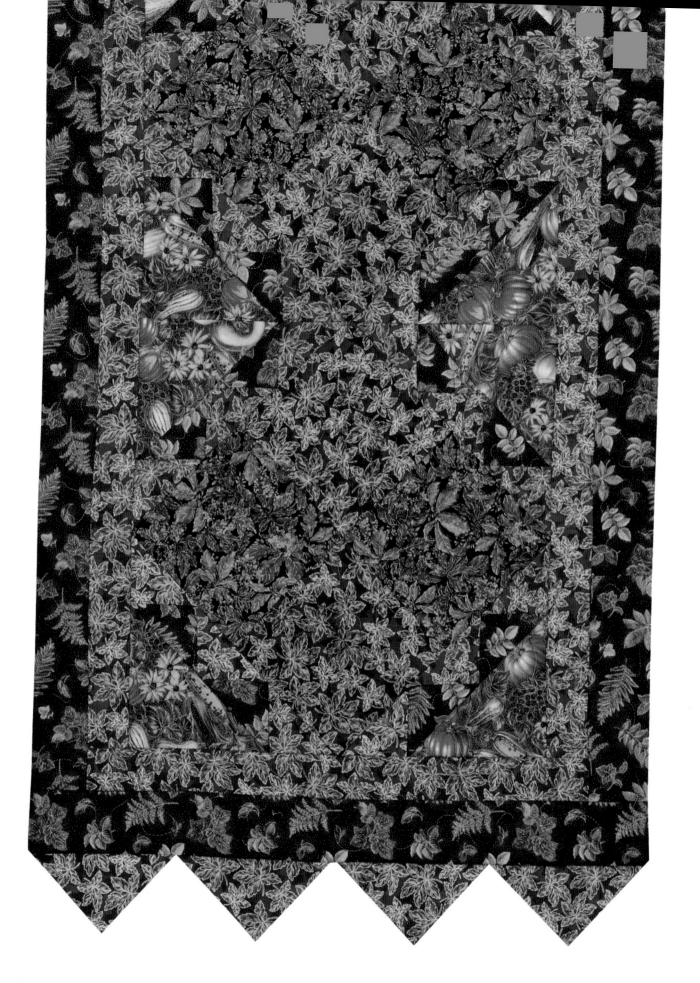

Fall Sensation

Designs by Carol Zentgraf

Not every quilt has to be cotton. This lovely traditional block pattern gives new life to velveteen, and the Euro shams make it a perfect fit for today's bed.

Project Notes

Velveteen has a nap—a pile or one-way direction in fabric that will take on different shades if not cut in the same direction. Consider the fabric nap when cutting all pieces to prevent color changes where they are not welcome.

Use double-sided basting tape instead of pins to prevent nap from shifting when sewing pieces together.

Press all seams after sewing as directed, using a press cloth on a towel or needle board to protect the nap.

Bed Runner

Project Specifications

Skill Level: Intermediate
Bed Runner Size: 69" x 30" without fringe
Block Size: 12" x 12"
Number of Blocks: 10

Petals
12" x 12" Block
Make 10 different-color
variations for bed runner
Make 2 different-color
variations for shams

Materials

Note: Velveteen fabric used in samples was 43" wide.
- 1¼ yards each burgundy, gold and rust velveteen
- 2 yards light green velveteen
- 2¼ yards dark green velveteen
- Fusible Fleece batting 69½" x 30½"
- All-purpose thread to match fabrics
- Rayon machine-embroidery thread to match fabrics and trim
- 4 yards lightweight fusible interfacing
- 10 (9" x 12) sheets paper-backed fusible web
- 2 yards gold tassel trim with decorative header
- Self-adhesive double-sided basting tape
- Template material
- Chalk pencil
- Gold 6-strand embroidery floss
- Long embroidery needle
- Press cloth
- Basic sewing tools and supplies

Cutting

Note: Because this fabric has a nap, mark the top of each strip, square or piece for ease of consistent nap placement later.

1. Cut two 3½" x 60½" B strips and two 5" x 30½" C strips light green velveteen along the length of the fabric.

2. Cut a 69½" x 30½" backing along the length of the dark green velveteen.

3. Following the manufacturer's instructions, apply fusible interfacing to the wrong side of the remaining length of the light green and dark green velveteen· and on ¾ yard of each of the remaining colors of velveteen.

4. Cut two 12½" A squares from each of the interfaced fabrics.

5. Prepare a template for the petal shape using the pattern given.

6. Trace four petal shapes onto the paper backing side of each sheet of fusible web to make a total of 40 petal shapes.

7. Referring to the manufacturer's instructions, fuse two traced sheets or a total of eight petals to the wrong side of the remainder of each interfaced fabric. Cut out shapes on traced lines and remove paper backing.

Completing the Blocks

1. Using a chalk pencil, draw diagonal lines from corner to corner on the right side of each A square.

2. Referring to Placement Diagram for color, select four same-color petals and one different-color A square.

3. Using the chalk lines as a guide for placement, arrange the four petals on A with the tips meeting in the center as shown in Figure 1.

Figure 1

4. Using a press cloth, fuse shapes in place.

5. Using the rayon thread to match the petals and a medium-wide zigzag stitch, sew around the edges of each petal to complete the block.

6. Repeat steps 2–5 with the remaining petals and A squares to make a total of 10 Petals blocks referring to the Placement Diagram for color combinations.

Completing the Bed Runner

1. Arrange and join the blocks to make two rows of five blocks each referring to the Placement Diagram for positioning of blocks; press seams in one direction.

2. Join the rows with seams facing in opposite directions.

3. Sew the B strips to opposite long sides of the pieced center, placing strips with the fabric nap going in the same direction; press seams toward strips. Sew the C strips to opposite ends as for B strips to complete the runner top; press seams toward strips.

4. Fuse the batting to the wrong side of the runner top.

5. Place the 69½" x 30½" backing rectangle right sides together with the fused runner top/batting layers; stitch along both long edges, leaving the short ends open.

6. Turn right side out; press long edges flat using a press cloth.

7. Finish short ends with a zigzag or overedge stitch or with a serger to hold.

8. Using a chalk pencil, mark a line through the center of each petal in each block.

9. Thread the long embroidery needle with 3 strands of gold embroidery floss; tie a knot at the end. Starting on the back side, stitch along the marked lines on each petal using a running stitch, stitching through all layers. Trim knotted ends.

10. Cut two 33" lengths of the tassel trim. Apply basting tape to the wrong side of each length.

11. Center and adhere a length of trim on each end of the runner, wrapping ends to the back side; topstitch the trim in place using thread to match the backing in the bobbin and thread to match the trim in the needle to finish.

Shams

Project Specifications

- Skill Level: Intermediate
- Sham Size: 26" x 26" without fringe
- Block Size: 12" x 12"
- Number of Blocks: 2

Materials

Note: *Velveteen fabric used in samples was 43" wide.*

- ½ yard gold velveteen
- 1¾ yards each burgundy and dark green velveteen
- All-purpose thread to match fabrics
- Rayon machine-embroidery thread to match fabrics
- 1 yard lightweight fusible interfacing
- 2 (9" x 12") sheets paper-backed fusible web
- ¼"-wide and ½"-wide fusible web tape
- 6 yards 3" gold bullion fringe with header
- 2 (26"-square) pillow forms
- Self-adhesive double-sided basting tape
- Template material
- Chalk pencil
- Gold 6-strand embroidery floss
- Long embroidery needle
- Press cloth
- Basic sewing tools and supplies

Cutting

Note: *Because this fabric has a nap, mark the top of each strip, square or piece for ease of consistent nap placement later.*

1. Cut four 7½" x 26½" B strips each burgundy and dark green velveteen along the length of the fabric.

2. Cut two 15" x 26½" pieces each burgundy and dark green velveteen for sham backs.

3. Following the manufacturer's instructions, apply fusible interfacing to the wrong side of the gold velveteen and 12" of the burgundy and dark green velveteen.

4. Cut two 12½" A squares from the gold interfaced fabric.

5. Prepare a template for the petal shape using the pattern given.

6. Trace four petal shapes onto the paper backing side of each sheet of fusible web for a total of eight petals.

7. Referring to the manufacturer's instructions, fuse one traced sheet to the wrong side of the burgundy and dark green interfaced fabric. Cut out shapes on traced lines and remove paper backing.

Completing the Blocks

1. Complete two Petals blocks referring to Completing the Blocks for the bed runner and to the Placement Diagrams for the shams.

2. Embroider the Petals blocks as in step 9 of Completing the Bed Runner.

Completing the Shams

1. Find the center of each Petals block and each B strip and mark with a pin.

2. Select four dark green B strips; center and sew a strip to each side of the gold/burgundy Petals block, placing strips with the fabric nap going in the same direction and stopping stitching ¼" from the end of the strip as shown in Figure 2.

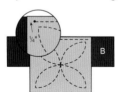

Figure 2

3. Fold the block on one diagonal with right sides together and align the border strips as shown in Figure 3; pin.

Figure 3

4. Using a clear straightedge and the chalk pencil, draw a line from the end of the stitching at one corner to the end of the B strips as shown in Figure 4.

Figure 4

5. Pin strips together perpendicular to the marked line; stitch on the line referring to Figure 5. Trim seam to ¼" and press mitered seams open.

Figure 5

6. Repeat steps 3–5 on each corner to complete the sham top.

7. Apply ¼"-wide fusible web tape around the edges of the completed sham top; remove paper backing and adhere the lower edge of the fringe header to the tape with fringe facing the inside.

8. Apply the ½"-wide fusible web tape to right long edge of the right side of one back rectangle and along the left long edge of the remaining rectangle. Remove paper backing and press the edges under ½" to hem.

9. Place the hemmed back rectangles right side up on a flat surface, overlapping the hemmed edges to make a 26½" square; pin to hold.

10. Place the completed sham top right sides together on top of the pinned back rectangles and pin to hold, being careful not to catch the fringe.

11. Stitch all around; clip corners. Turn right side out through the overlap and press.

12. Insert pillow form to finish.

13. Repeat steps 2–11 to complete the second sham using the remaining Petals block and back pieces. ■

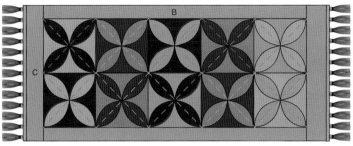

Fall Sensation Bed Runner
Placement Diagram
69" x 30" without fringe

Burgundy Fall Sensation Pillow Sham
Placement Diagram
26" x 26" without fringe

Green Fall Sensation Pillow Sham
Placement Diagram
26" x 26" without fringe

Petal
Cut 8 each rust, gold, dark green, light green & burgundy
velveteen with nap going in one direction for bed runner
Cut 4 each burgundy & dark green velveteen with nap
going in one direction for shams

House of White Birches, Berne, Indiana 46711   Clotilde.com

Winter Wonderland

Designs by Nancy McNally

This bed runner and sham set will be the focal point of any room. Top your bed with a wonderland of soft blues.

Project Specifications
Skill Level: Intermediate
Bed Runner Size: 97½" x 40½"
Sham Sizes: 23" x 23" and 25" x 25"
Block Size: 7½" x 7½"
Number of Blocks: 33

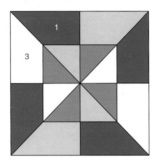

Framed Pinwheel
7½" x 7½" Block
Make 16

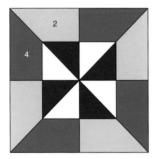

Reverse Framed Pinwheel
7½" x 7½" Block
Make 17

Materials
- 1¼ yards total dark blue batiks
- 1¾ yards total light blue batiks
- 1¾ yards total bright blue batiks
- 1⅞ yards total medium blue batiks
- 2 yards muslin
- 4¼ yards white solid
- Backing 106" x 49"

- Batting: 106" x 49" (runner), 31" x 31" (sham 1), 33" x 33" (sham 2)
- Neutral-color all-purpose thread
- Quilting thread
- Template material
- 1 pillow form each 22" and 24" square
- Basic sewing tools and supplies

Cutting

1. Prepare templates for A/B, E, F, G, H, K and M pieces using patterns given; cut all, except the A/B pieces, as directed on each piece.

2. Cut (17) 2½" by fabric width A strips total white solid and light blue batiks.

3. Cut (17) 2½" by fabric width B strips total medium blue, bright blue and dark blue batiks.

4. Cut one 8" by fabric width strip medium blue batik; subcut strip into two 8" N squares. Trim the remainder of the strip to 6¼" and subcut strip into three 6¼" squares. Cut each 6¼" square on both diagonals to make a total of 12 J triangles.

5. Cut three 2½" by fabric width strips medium blue batik; subcut strips into (40) 2½" D squares.

6. Cut one 2½" by fabric width strip each medium and bright blue batiks; subcut each strip into two 2½" x 15½" O strips.

7. Cut two 2½" by fabric width strips white solid; subcut strips into four 2½" x 15½" P strips.

8. Cut five 8" by fabric width strips white solid; subcut strips into (66) 2½" x 8" C strips. Trim the remainder of the leftover strip to 5½" and subcut into four 5½" R squares.

9. Cut one 5½" by fabric width strip each medium blue and bright blue batiks; subcut each strip into two 5½" x 15½" S strips.

10. Cut one 11⅜" by fabric width strip each medium and bright blue batiks; subcut each strip into one 11⅜" square. Cut each square on both diagonals to make four I triangles each fabric; set aside two medium blue I triangles for another project.

11. Cut one each 31" square and 33" square muslin for sham-top backings.

12. Cut two 15" x 23½" rectangles white solid for back for sham 1.

13. Cut two 16" x 25½" rectangles white solid for sham 2 back.

14. Cut one 6¼" square from the leftover white solid; cut the square on both diagonals to make a total of four L triangles.

15. Cut one 4½" by fabric width strip light blue batik; subcut strip into four 4½" Q squares.

16. Cut enough 2¼"-wide strips from leftover blue batiks to equal 290" when joined for binding.

Completing the Blocks

1. Select one A strip and one B strip; join with right sides together along length. Press seam toward A. Repeat to make a total of 17 A-B strip sets.

2. Prepare a template for A-B using the pattern given.

3. Place the template right side up on an A-B strip set, placing dot-dash line on seam, and cut a unit 1 as shown in Figure 1; turn the template and cut a unit 2, again referring to Figure 1. Repeat across the strip set to cut eight each units 1 and 2 from the strip. Repeat with additional strip sets to cut a total of 64 each units 1 and 2.

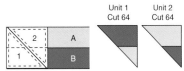

Unit 1
Cut 64

Unit 2
Cut 64

Figure 1

4. Flip the template back side up and place it on an A-B strip set to cut a unit 3 as shown in Figure 2; turn the flipped template and cut a unit 4. Repeat across the strip set and with additional strip sets to cut a total of 64 each units 3 and 4.

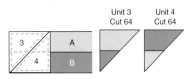

Unit 3
Cut 64

Unit 4
Cut 64

Figure 2

5. Place the template right side up on an A-B strip set to cut a unit 2 as shown in Figure 3; flip the template back side up and turn it to cut a unit 4, again referring to Figure 3. Continue to cut units 2 and 4 across the strip set to cut a total of four each units 2 and 4 from the strip set. You will need a total of 68 each units 2 and 4 from this step and steps 3 and 4.

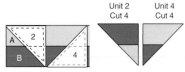

Unit 2
Cut 4

Unit 4
Cut 4

Figure 3

6. To complete one Framed Pinwheel block, select four each assorted units 1 and 3.

Tips & Techniques

You may eliminate the need for a template by using the Easy Angle Ruler on the strips. To save time, you may layer two strips with wrong sides together, alternating placement of the colors, to cut units 1 and 3 at the same time, and units 2 and 4 at the same time. The completed blocks will then be trimmed to 8" x 8".

7. Sew a unit 1 to a unit 3 to complete a block quarter as shown in Figure 4; press seam to one side. Repeat to complete a total of four block quarters.

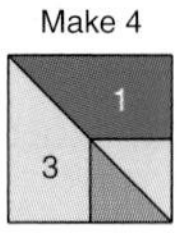

Make 4

Figure 4

8. Join two block quarters to make a row as shown in Figure 5; press seam to one side. Repeat to make a second row.

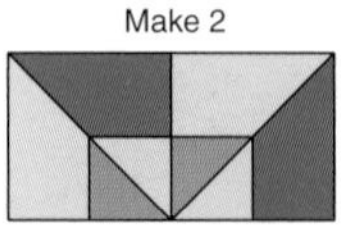

Make 2

Figure 5

9. Join the rows as shown in Figure 6 to complete one Framed Pinwheel block; press seam to one side.

Make 16

Figure 6

10. Repeat steps 6–9 to complete a total of 16 Framed Pinwheel blocks.

11. Repeat steps 6–10 using units 2 and 4 to make 17 Reverse Framed Pinwheel blocks as shown in Figure 7.

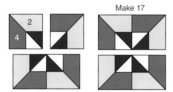

Make 17

Figure 7

Completing the Quilt

1. Select and join a total of nine blocks (mixing both Framed Pinwheel and Reverse Framed Pinwheel blocks) and 10 C strips to make a block row as shown in Figure 8; press seams toward C strips. Repeat to make a total of three block rows.

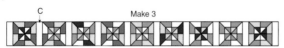

C   Make 3

Figure 8

2. Select and join nine C strips and 10 D squares to make a sashing row as shown in Figure 9; press seams toward D squares. Repeat to make a total of four sashing rows.

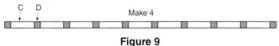

C D   Make 4

Figure 9

3. Join the sashing rows with the block rows, beginning and ending with a sashing row referring to the Placement Diagram, to complete the pieced center; press seams toward sashing rows.

4. Sew an F piece to two adjacent sides of H to make an F-H unit as shown in Figure 10; press seams toward F. Repeat to make four F-H units.

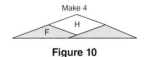

Make 4

Figure 10

5. Sew an E piece to one short side of an F piece to make an E-F unit. Repeat to make a second E-F unit as shown in Figure 11.

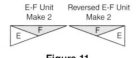

E-F Unit   Reversed E-F Unit
Make 2   Make 2

Figure 11

6. Repeat step 5 with the remaining E and F pieces to make two reversed E-F units, again referring to Figure 11.

7. Join two F-H units with three G pieces and add an E-F unit to the left end and a reversed E-F unit to the right end to complete one side strip as shown in Figure 12; press seams toward G. Repeat to make a second side strip.

Make 2

Figure 12

8. Sew a side strip to opposite sides of the pieced center referring to the Placement Diagram for positioning of strips; press seams toward the sashing strips.

9. Sew a J triangle to two adjacent sides of K to make a J-K unit as shown in Figure 13; press seams toward J. Repeat to make a total of four J-K units.

Make 4

Figure 13

10. Sew J to L to make a J-L unit as shown in Figure 14; press seam toward J. Repeat to make a second J-L unit and two reversed J-L units, again referring to Figure 14.

Reversed
J-L Unit   J-L Unit
Make 2   Make 2

Figure 14

11. Arrange and join three I triangles with two J-K units and add a J-L unit to one end and a reversed J-L unit to the opposite end to complete one end strip as shown in Figure 15; press seams toward I. Repeat to make a second end strip.

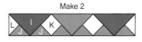

Make 2

Figure 15

House of White Birches, Berne, Indiana 46711   Clotilde.com

12. Sew an M square to each end of each end strip and sew these strips to opposite short ends of the pieced center to complete the runner top; press seams toward M and then toward the sashing rows.

13. Sandwich the batting rectangle between the completed runner top and the prepared backing piece; pin or baste layers together to hold. Quilt as desired by hand or machine.

14. When quilting is complete, trim batting and backing fabric even with raw edges of the runner top.

15. Join binding strips on short ends with diagonal seams to make one long strip as shown in Figure 16; trim seams to ¼" and press seams open.

Figure 16

16. Fold the binding strip with wrong sides together along length; press.

17. Sew binding to the runner edges, mitering corners and overlapping ends. Fold binding to the back side and stitch in place to finish the bed runner.

Completing Sham 1

1. To complete sham 1, select two Framed Pinwheel blocks, two N squares and four each O, P and Q pieces. ***Note:*** *Use whatever blocks you have leftover from making the bed runner.*

2. Referring to the Placement Diagram throughout, sew a block to an N square to make a row; repeat to make a second row. Press seams toward N. Join the rows to complete the pieced center; press seam to one side.

3. Sew an O strip to a P strip; press seam toward O. Repeat to make a total of four O-P strips.

4. Sew an O-P strip to opposite sides of the pieced center with O strips toward the inside as shown in Figure 17; press seams toward the strips.

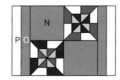

Figure 17

5. Sew a Q square to each end of each remaining O-P strip; press seam away from Q. Sew these strips to the remaining sides of the pieced center to complete the sham top; press seams toward strips.

6. Sandwich the 31"-square batting between the completed sham top and the muslin 31" backing square; pin or baste layers together to hold. Quilt as desired by hand or machine.

7. When quilting is complete, trim batting and muslin even with raw edges of the sham top.

8. Turn under one 23½" edge of each 15" x 23½" white solid back rectangle ¼" and press. Turn under ½"; press and stitch to hem.

9. Layer the hemmed back rectangles right sides together with the quilted sham top, matching the unhemmed edges and overlapping the hemmed edges as shown in Figure 18; stitch all around.

Figure 18

10. Turn right side out through the opening and insert the 22" pillow form to finish.

Completing Sham 2

1. To complete sham 2, select the four remaining Framed Pinwheel blocks, four S strips and four R squares.

2. Referring to the Placement Diagram throughout, join two of the remaining blocks to make a row; press seam to one side. Repeat to make a second row. Join the rows to complete the pieced center; press seam to one side.

3. Sew an S strip to opposite sides of the pieced center; press seams toward strips.

4. Sew an R square to each end of each remaining S strip; press seam away from R. Sew these strips to the remaining sides of the pieced center to complete the sham top; press seams toward strips.

5. Sandwich the 33"-square batting between the completed sham top and the muslin 33" backing square; pin or baste layers together to hold. Quilt as desired by hand or machine.

6. When quilting is complete, trim batting and muslin even with raw edges of the sham top.

7. Turn under one 25½" edge of each 16" x 25½" white solid back rectangle ¼" and press. Turn under ½" press and stitch to hem.

8. Layer the hemmed back rectangles right sides together with the quilted sham top, matching the unhemmed edges and overlapping the hemmed edges, again referring to Figure 18; stitch all around.

9. Turn right side out through the opening and insert the 24" pillow form to finish. ■

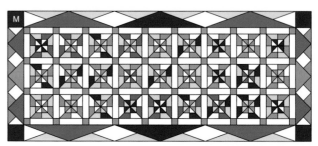

Winter Wonderland Bed Runner
Placement Diagram
97½" x "40½"

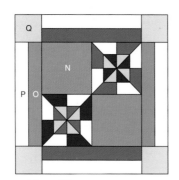

Winter Wonderland Sham 1
Placement Diagram
23" x 23"

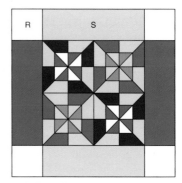

Winter Wonderland Sham 2
Placement Diagram
25" x 25"

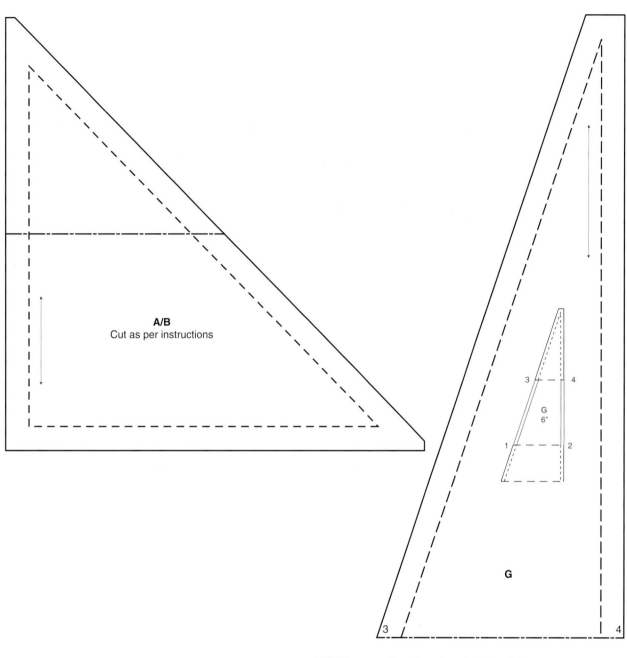

A/B
Cut as per instructions

G

G
6"

Add 6" between G sections to make G template

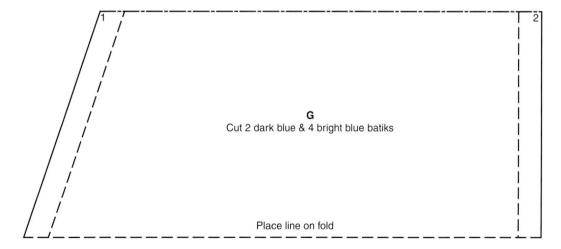

G
Cut 2 dark blue & 4 bright blue batiks

Place line on fold

House of White Birches, Berne, Indiana 46711   Clotilde.com

56

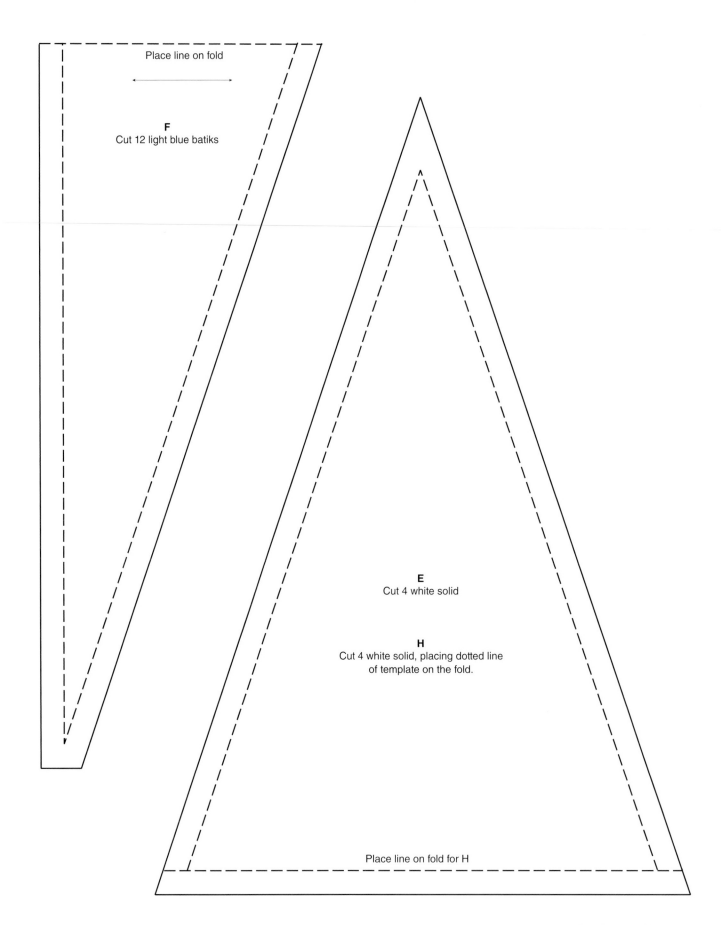

Place line on fold

F
Cut 12 light blue batiks

E
Cut 4 white solid

H
Cut 4 white solid, placing dotted line
of template on the fold.

Place line on fold for H

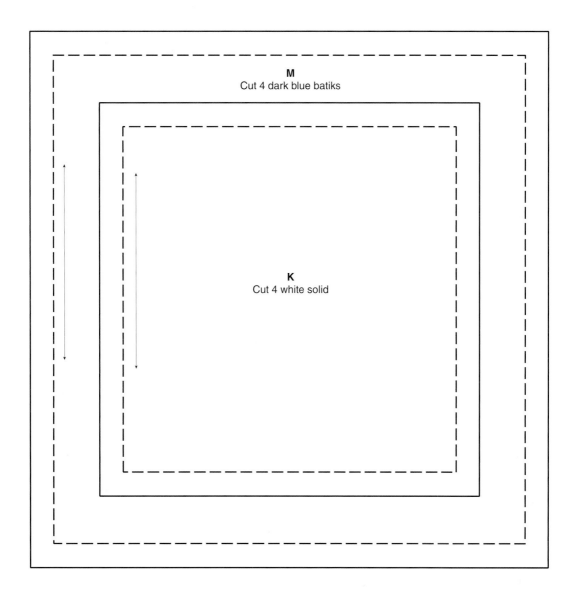

Holiday Fantasy

Design by Nancy McNally

Deck the halls and your bed with this appliquéd bed runner.
It will add the perfect touch to any bedroom during the holidays.

Project Specifications
Skill Level: Confident Beginner
Bed Runner Size: 101" x 43"
Block Size: 12½" x 12½"
Number of Blocks: 6

Holiday Fantasy
12½" x 12½" Block
Make 6

Materials
Note: All fabrics have gold metallic in the prints.
• ½ yard green print
• 1½ yards burgundy print
• 1⅔ yards cream reindeer print
• 2¼ yards cream print
• Backing 109" x 52"
• Batting 109" x 52"
• All-purpose thread to match fabrics
• Quilting thread
• 2¼ yards 18"-wide fusible web
• Chalk pencil
• Basic sewing tools and supplies

Cutting
1. Cut four 13" by fabric width strips cream print; subcut strips into (12) 13" A squares.

2. Cut seven 2¼" by fabric width strips cream print for binding.

3. Cut two 13" by fabric width strips burgundy print; subcut strips into (32) 2½" x 13" B strips.

4. Cut eight 6½" by fabric width D/E strips cream reindeer print.

5. Cut two 2½" by fabric width strips green print; subcut strips into (21) 2½" C squares.

6. Trace appliqué pieces onto the paper side of the fusible web as directed on each piece for number to cut, leaving ½" between pieces.

7. Cut out shapes, leaving a margin around each piece. Fuse shapes to the wrong side of fabrics as directed on each piece for color; cut out shapes on traced lines. Remove paper backing.

Completing the Blocks
1. Fold and crease six A squares horizontally, vertically and diagonally to mark the centers.

2. Select one creased A square, one center, eight petals, four each leaves and flowers and 28 berries for one block.

3. Arrange and fuse the pieces on the A square in numerical order referring to the pattern, block drawing and creased lines on A for positioning.

4. When all pieces have been fused in place, use matching thread to straight-stitch close to the edges of all pieces, except berries, to secure and complete one block.

5. Repeat steps 1–4 to complete a total of six appliquéd Holiday Fantasy blocks.

Completing the Bed Runner
1. Select and join three A squares, three appliquéd Holiday Fantasy blocks and seven B strips to make an X row as shown in Figure 1; press seams toward B strips

X Row

Figure 1

2. Select and join three A squares, three appliquéd Holiday Fantasy blocks and seven B strips to make a Y row as shown in Figure 2; press seams toward B strips.

Y Row

Figure 2

3. Select and join six B strips and seven C squares to make a sashing row as shown in Figure 3. Press seams toward B strips. Repeat to make a total of three sashing rows.

C   B   Make 3

Figure 3

4. Join the X and Y rows with the sashing rows to complete the pieced center referring to the Placement Diagram; press seams toward sashing rows.

5. Join the D/E strips on the short ends to make one long strip; press seams open. Subcut the strip into two 6½" x 47" D strips and two 6½" x 106" E strips.

6. Center and sew a D strip to each short end and E strips to the long sides of the pieced center, starting and stopping stitching ¼" from each corner of the pieced center as shown in Figure 4.

Figure 4

7. Fold one corner of the pieced center at a 45-degree angle with right sides together and align the border strips as shown in Figure 5; pin.

Figure 5

8. Using a clear straightedge and the chalk pencil, draw a line from the end of the stitching at one corner to the end of the border strips as shown in Figure 6.

Figure 6

9. Pin strips together perpendicular to the marked line; stitch on the line referring to Figure 7. Trim seam to ¼" and press mitered seams open; press D and E seams toward the strips.

Figure 7

10. Repeat steps 7–9 on each corner to complete the runner top.

11. Sandwich the batting rectangle between the completed runner top and the prepared backing piece; pin or baste layers together to hold. Quilt as desired by hand or machine.

12. When quilting is complete, trim batting and backing fabric even with raw edges of the runner top.

13. Join binding strips on short ends with diagonal seams to make one long strip as shown in Figure 8; trim seams to ¼" and press seams open.

Figure 8

14. Fold the binding strip with wrong sides together along length; press.

15. Sew binding to the runner top edges, mitering corners and overlapping ends. Fold binding to the back side and stitch in place to finish the bed runner. ∎

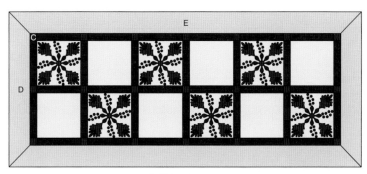

Holiday Fantasy
Placement Diagram
101" x 43"

House of White Birches, Berne, Indiana 46711   Clotilde.com

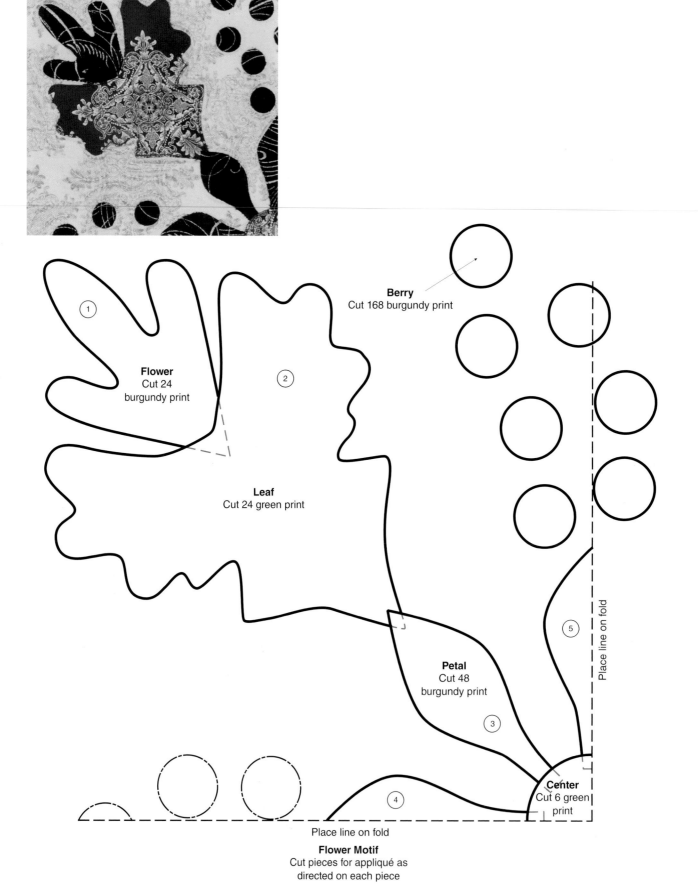

Berry
Cut 168 burgundy print

Flower
Cut 24
burgundy print

1

2

Leaf
Cut 24 green print

Petal
Cut 48
burgundy print

3

4

5

Place line on fold

Center
Cut 6 green
print

Place line on fold

Flower Motif
Cut pieces for appliqué as
directed on each piece

Finishing Your Bed Runner or Sham

Step 1. Sandwich the batting between the completed top and prepared backing; pin or baste layers together to hold. *Note: If using basting spray to hold layers together, refer to instructions on the product container for use.*

Step 2. Quilt as desired by hand or machine; remove pins or basting. Trim excess backing and batting even with quilt top.

Step 3. Join binding strips on short ends to make one long strip. Fold the strip in half along length with wrong sides together; press.

Step 4. Sew binding to quilt edges, mitering corners and overlapping ends. Fold binding to the back side and stitch in place to finish. ▪

Fabric & Supplies

Fall Sensation: Soft-Touch pillow forms from Fairfield Processing Corp.; featherweight fusible interfacing and fusible batting from Pellon; Collins Wonder Tape basting tape from Prym Consumer USA; Toscana Velveteen fabrics provided by Robert Kaufman; tassel trim No. IR2567BR and gimp trim No. IR2688BR provided by A Treasure Nest; Steam-A-Seam 2 fusible web tape and sheets from The Warm Company.

Pineapple Pleasures: Tri-Recs Tri Tool and Recs Tool ruler/templates from EZ Quilting by Wrights.

Summer Blossoms: Cotton batting and Steam-A-Seam 2 fusible web from The Warm Company; Blendables multicolored cotton thread from Sulky; Penny Lane fabric collection from Quilting Treasures by Cranston.

Celebration: Poly-Fil Low-Loft quilt batting from Fairfield Processing Corp.; Kona cotton solids and Pimatex prints from Robert Kaufman.

Geometric Jazz: Poly-Fil Low-Loft quilt batting from Fairfield Processing Corp.; muslin provided by James Thompson. Free Spirit solid-color fabrics and Rowan Kaffe Fassett prints provided by Westminster Fibers.

Holiday Fantasy: Holiday Splendor fabric collection from Hoffman California Fabrics; Sulky threads.

Warm Splendor: Cotton batting from The Warm Company; Blendables multicolored cotton thread from Sulky; Cornucopia fabric collection from Quilting Treasures by Cranston. ▪

HOUSE of WHITE BIRCHES
PUBLISHERS SINCE 1947

Bed Runners & More is published by DRG, 306 East Parr Road, Berne, IN 46711. Printed in USA. Copyright © 2012 DRG. All rights reserved. This publication may not be reproduced in part or in whole without written permission from the publisher.

RETAIL STORES: If you would like to carry this pattern book or any other DRG publications, visit DRGwholesale.com

Every effort has been made to ensure that the instructions in this pattern book are complete and accurate. We cannot, however, take responsibility for human error, typographical mistakes or variations in individual work. Please visit ClotildeCustomerCare.com to check for pattern updates.

ISBN: 978-1-59217-373-0

1 2 3 4 5 6 7 8 9

Photo Index

3

10

18

25

32

38

42

48

59